A MANIFESTO FOR AMERICANS

THE A.N.S.W.E.R.

G. SIDNEY NORDÉ

PLUS M.O.S.E.S. & ALIENS.

Edited by Rhonda Lee Thomas

TABLE OF CONTENTS

A MANIFESTO FOR AMERICANS

ACKNOWLEDGMENTS

PREFACE

A Manifesto For Americans

Dedicated to two Kings and one man; the first King committed his entire adult life to spread a message that the second King summed up in six words — "Can't we all just get along?" Then the man championed a campaign to answer both Kings at once... "Yes, We Can."

PUBLIC ACKNOWLEDGMENTS

These newsworthy individuals listed below mentioned some belief, action, concept, or quip that I found to be totally in line with what I suggest in *THE ANSWER*. Their words and actions were light along a path of certainty as I crafted this work. I felt it fitting to acknowledge how these folks, even though I don't know them personally, greatly contributed to this manifesto. The ultimate solution I espouse is multifaceted, but when broken down to its individual components it will address each of the issues, I heard these people speak about. Please, see for yourself what I heard them say or do, plus my immediate response, and after you read *THE ANSWER*, you may acknowledge them as well.

His Royal Highness Crown Prince Al Hussein bin Abdullah of Jordan – overheard giving a speech at the 2020 Annual TechWadi Silicon Valley tech conference: "Our young, talented workforce is hungry for careers in technology." I remember thinking "If he reads *THE ANSWER*, he can make jobs for every young person in his country!"

Bill Ackman – a billionaire NYC hedge fund manager quoted online at businessinsider.com that the government could and should give students a $6,750 investment account at birth and by retirement it would be worth an approximate one million dollars. I remember thinking, "Yes, that is exactly what I'm writing about, and I know just where to get the money from… NOT the government though!"

Michael Bloomberg – a billionaire and former NYC mayor who appointed a business executive in 2011 to overhaul the city school system to function more like a business. I remember thinking as I wrote *THE ANSWER* in 2020, "Bloomberg tried this years ago, he was on to something!" Donald Trump, also a billionaire, and former U.S. President who appointed a business executive in 2017 to overhaul the nation's school system to function more like a business. I remember thinking in 2017 "Bloomberg tried this years ago, he was on to something!"

Charles Blow – a journalist for the *New York Times*, authored "The Devil You Know: A Black Power Manifesto" in 2020. I remember thinking "Wow, another 'black' man in America has written a manifesto during the pandemic!" I must be on to something!"

Ruby Bridges – iconic Civil Rights legend known for integrating "white" elementary school as first "black" student, overheard in 2020 during documentary interview: "We can teach people how to NOT be racist." I remember thinking, "Yes Ruby! And if we pay them to learn…!?"

Alexandria Ocasio Cortez – a U.S. Congresswoman who advocates for a Green New Deal, a plan to incorporate cleaner technologies to promote economic growth. I remember thinking "Wow! The AOC sounds like FDR's New Deal! But instead of 'clean' Green, what about 'mean' Green? And if we use cryptocurrency, it would be a 'Mean-Green-Clean-New Deal!'"

The Honorable John Lewis – a distinguished U.S. Congressman who dedicated his life to the Civil Rights movement overheard during 2020 saying the younger generation and young people will be instrumental in the solution to address cultural, ethnic, and racial hatred. I remember thinking "Yes, we can teach them how, using the schools! Thank you, Congressman!"

Zoe McCall – 15 years old, a self-described activist and entrepreneur overheard testifying before the Board of Education in Prince George's County, Maryland about the importance of financial education for students. I remember thinking "That's exactly what I'm writing about! She should be ON the Board of Education, not testifying before it."

NAS – award-winning hip-hop artist overheard on a panel discussion about racial tension and conflict: "I'm not sure what the solution is, but when I hear it, I'll know." I remember thinking, "I hope he'll hear about THE ANSWER and know this is it!"

Andrew Yang – a U.S. presidential, and NYC mayoral candidate whose campaign platform was a Universal Basic Income of $1,000 monthly for American citizens. I thought, "Great idea! I wonder what he would think about paying students with cryptocurrency and allowing parents to access their earnings.. Let me finish *THE ANSWER*."

PERSONAL ACKNOWLEDGMENTS

Thank you to my parents! **Lolo Smith** and **"Doc" Nordé** for being exemplary, through your generosity to the community, and the near blueprint-like groundwork of career paths you both blazed in the fields of non-profit, education, and authorship; the same paths I chose! Go figure.

My editor, **Rhonda Thomas**, and graphic designer, **Gloria Marconi**! Thank you for mastering your crafts, for the education, and the conversation. Look! I got a book!

And **Marcus Harris** of New York City by way of Texas and Puerto Rico! Thank you for the "lightbulb" moment and chewing my ear off about bitcoin and blockchain. Now, I can chew everyone else's ear too.

PREFACE

A quick note, then some details about the layout of the manifesto.

Ironic, but the 2020 pandemic actually solved some problems. Personally, one of my biggest pet peeves vanished during COVID; walking into public establishments, like a fast-food restaurant, with multiple checkout lines of varying lengths. I prefer how banks have one line where everyone waits for the next available teller. This means consistently shorter wait times at the bank, versus long waits at stores with inefficient line management. Now, coming out of the pandemic and slowly going back to "normal," we also risk going backwards to those outdated, inefficient ways of doing things.

This is the vein in which this manifesto was written; like an old relationship we should NOT go back to. Relationships are meant for us to gain knowledge, through success AND failures, so that we can then enter NEW relationships and build prior knowledge into wisdom. America needs to break up with the past, not miss it, but keep fond memories to comfort us before our new relationship with the future. Keep in mind, the future will become old too and we will need to break up again. What do we do then...?

WELCOME to *THE ANSWER!*

This work is presented in two parts. The first section, a guidebook, is part manifesto and government proposal. It guides the reader through a proposed solution (*T.H.E. A.N.S.W.E.R.*) for reforming American society via our educational system. The second section, "Headlines from the Teen New Deal," is a collection of fictional headlines telling the story of what could happen on the road to implementing *T.H.E. A.N.S.W.E.R.*

The guidebook has six chapters. It is written as one extended piece however, with an introduction and conclusion titled "The Known" and "The Unknown." The intervening four chapters represent the past, present, future, and beyond, with their own respective titles: A\Way It Was Done; A\Way Until Now; A\Way Forward; and A\Way. All of the chapters are very short, the longest two being those representing the future and beyond. *T.H.E. A.N.S.W.E.R.* is presented in A\Way Forward, the fourth chapter, the future. It is not immediately in the beginning as to put forth a larger message. We often wish to instantly have the rewards of the future but we cannot truly appreciate them without journeying from our past and through our present dilemma to achieve the rewards we seek. The fifth chapter, A\Way (Beyond), includes other potential reforms that should present themselves upon implementing the solution. M.O.S.E.S. and A.L.I.E.N.S. are examples of these possible reforms.

The title of the four main chapters presenting "A\Way" with a slash points to a double meaning: (1) the goal of our nation is to get "away" from our current predicament – a long-standing history of ethnic/racial inequities, conflict, and other injustices pervading our society, and (2) *T.H.E. A.N.S.W.E.R.* is "a way" we can achieve the goal of stemming the tide of injustice and undesirable human behaviors. Simply put, the suggestion contained herein is a way we can get away from our present dilemma.

Thank you for reading and participating in this short journey from our past into our future and beyond. Now, let's begin with what we know.

CHAPTER

INTRODUCTION (THE KNOWN)

Now we know that we are stuck. We are stuck in the presence of a global pandemic that is halting our normal routines and stifling our economy and we are stuck in a cycle of inequity and injustice steeped in racial tension, police brutality, civil unrest, and socioeconomic disparities. How we get unstuck is the obvious question. How we get unstuck from two completely different problems is something totally different, but there is one group of Americans who can lead us out of both scenarios, one group of Americans that represent *T.H.E. A.N.S.W.E.R.* Guess who.

We know that with the pandemic, only some of the solution is clear because the medical community has had some preparation responding to other outbreaks. But the medical community cannot address the effects of drastic job loss and unemployment associated with the pandemic. Nor can they provide the remedy needed for socioeconomic disparities resulting from inequity and injustice present before the inception of our nation.

We know that, because this inequity and injustice has been present from the very beginning, it indicates that our nation is not complete. The founding documents of our nation say, "all men are created equal," and our laws tell us the administration of justice will be fair and free from prejudice; yet we are not there—we are stuck between the lines. Unless we come up with a real and lasting solution, the dream of America that the founders envisioned is on track to fail.

We know that America is the "Disney World" of nations, welcome and open to everyone, but it is a business nonetheless exemplified by the capitalistic structure of our economy. All "Disney World's customers," the American citizens, naturalized and otherwise, are not all treated fairly, so we should consider our nearly 250 year history of being in business as our soft launch. It is time for us to iron out the kinks and handle serious business that has been overlooked way too long by design.

We know that when prosperous businesses falter, they use 20/20 hindsight to look for signs that point to a solution. Here are three precedents that have been set, signs pointing to the obvious solution that awaits us in the future:

CHILD LABOR

According to the United Nations' International Children's Emergency Fund, in the least-developed nations, more than 25 percent of children between the ages of 5–17 are engaged in forms of child labor, much of it forced, which poses serious risks to their health and development.

The sign is… child labor.

SUMMER YOUTH EMPLOYMENT PROGRAMS

According to the Brookings Institution, some of the largest cities in America annually employ hundreds of thousands of young people between the ages of 14–24 in Summer Youth Employment Programs. Some of those programs have been in operation for decades in places like the District of Columbia and New York City. Youth employment is a benefit to the communities and families of those young people who work. Yet, the youth unemployment rate is staggering.

The sign is teen employment.

PRIVATIZING EDUCATION

For years there has been a push to encourage public schools and school systems to adopt a more business-minded approach to their operations. Former New York City Mayor Michael Bloomberg appointed a business executive as chancellor of the city's school system during his term in office. Former President Donald Trump selected a businesswoman as U.S. Secretary of Education. Neither appointee accomplished great success in the move toward privatization, but the call to action cannot be ignored.

The sign is... schools as businesses.

So... child labor + youth employment + schools as businesses = ???

We know these signs point to a solution; but what is it? Up until this point, we have not had to create a solution, but now we must! The looming threat of another pandemic is larger than ever because of the ease with which people travel the world. We must also acknowledge the potential greater threat from within our own borders due to domestic terror, racial hatred, and other evils. With the global pandemic, we are offered a glaring opportunity to pause, look at ourselves in the mirror, reflect on our past together as one country "business," and improve our youth and our future.

This can be achieved by looking to the past and revisiting a solution in which a segment of the American populace was excluded from decision making abilities...

CHAPTER

A\WAY IT WAS DONE (THE PAST)

...more than 80 years ago when President Franklin D. Roosevelt and his administration enacted a series of social and government programs known collectively as the "New Deal." It was an answer that provided temporary and permanent solutions for millions of Americans in a broad stroke of sweeping change between the years 1933–1939. By having the programs introduced over a longer period, it ensured the federal government's commitment to addressing the underlying problems in a strategic, orderly, and genuine manner. Even though there were millions of people desperate for recovery and relief, seeing continuous government reform over several years provided hope and reassurance that positive change was guaranteed.

The medical community will not and cannot solve the global pandemic overnight. Health experts and organizations look at what success they have had previously dealing with these situations, then cautiously move forward to provide smarter healing methods. Likewise, social inequity and injustice will not be erased instantly. We must examine our previous accomplishments for A\WAY to navigate through uncharted and troubled waters over a carefully calculated period of time, like the New Deal solutions were implemented.

It took a while, but Americans began to experience the positive benefits of the New Deal. However, one age group still has not been on the receiving end of benefits although they are just like every other group in America that does. That age group is living in desperate situations, including random gun violence, racism, climate change, and other social ills, just like every other group in America. That age group has been denied a voice altogether. The desperation of that group had already existed long before the pandemic and throughout generation after generation of racial conflict. Their voice has been suppressed because of their age.

If we would offer them a voice, a new New Deal—a meaningful deal to enter the vocal section of our society—that is enacted over the course of several years...

CHAPTER

A\WAY UNTIL NOW (THE PRESENT)

... perhaps we can put the finishing touches on our great nation by healing old wounds and stamping out racial hatred to create an actual democracy.

Although all of the old New Deal programs did not endure, many of them did. Arguably the most important program to last is the Social Security Act of 1935. Until now, it has been A\ WAY to permanently provide universal retirement and pension funds (for Americans who worked) and unemployment insurance (for Americans who worked). Did you notice the pattern there? Americans who worked.

The Social Security portion of the New Deal is a tremendous success that offers ongoing solutions for millions of working Americans. If you are allowed to work, Social Security will work for you. If you are allowed to work, you are allowed to vote. If you are allowed to vote, you are allowed to have a voice.

Two New Deal programs did not provide lasting benefits like the Social Security system: the Fair Labor Standards Act (FLSA) of 1938 and the National Youth Administration of 1935, which was initially begun to educate and provide jobs for youth. FLSA made it expressly forbidden for youth under age 16 to work. The National Youth Administration was disbanded in 1943 after only 8 years. Now there are millions of Americans who are not allowed to work, not allowed to contribute to our economy, not allowed a vote or a voice, but who are in desperate situations where change is required. Now there are millions of Americans who were initially in the deal but then got cut out. This is how the New Deal has become an old deal.

A new New Deal is mandatory! One of our loftiest social accomplishments, the Social Security program, is in danger of losing funds soon unless there is reform. Politicians continue to propose legislation like, or inspired by, the old New Deal. Senator Bernie Sanders has proposed legislation to make colleges and universities tuition free but, considering that we already have free primary and secondary education that is quite unequal, extending this to higher education seems even more inequitable and unjust.

Representative Alexandria Ocasio-Cortez, Senator Ed Markey, and others have proposed a "Green New Deal" aiming to address climate change and socioeconomic inequality and injustice with ideas like renewable energy and resource efficiency.

These new proposals have been received with some fanfare, but they do not address many pressing needs, suggest a permanent fix for Social Security, nor do they offer direct or immediate benefits to a group of millions of Americans desperate for change. Most of these citizens are patriotically contributing to our society, but have never held jobs; have an opinion, but have never had the opportunity to vote; must face the uncertainty of random gun violence, racism, the looming cloud of climate change, and other social ills every day, but must fight to be heard.

These Americans with no voice, yet who simultaneously hold the key to unlocking the true strength of our nation are...

CHAPTER

A\WAY FORWARD (THE FUTURE)

...young people—children and teenagers—the one group of marginalized Americans who are not allowed to work or vote, but who could lead our nation to a future with diminished social ills plus an economy strong enough to propel us out of the pandemic and back onto a path to solidify real democracy! How?

Youth, especially children, are usually not as biased and prejudiced as adults and they are more trusting and open-minded. While young and impressionable, society should incentivize, reward, and compensate youth to maintain morally upright behavior as students into early adulthood. Slowly but surely, America would transform via the kind of people that we produce academically and socially.

The pandemic instantly unemployed droves of Americans, many from jobs that cannot be done remotely. The labor of tens of millions of people suddenly vanished! However, almost unscathed by the pandemic, the educational community banded together to keep schools, and around 50 million students (perhaps an untapped labor pool), "in business" online. If students were compensated for their online academic work and associated activities, those earnings could be passed on to adult family members, particularly during future pandemics and other national emergencies.

We must not continue to miseducate and produce problematic children who grow up to become problematic adults who produce more of the same deep-rooted hate, inequities, and injustices that consume us. By consistently incentivizing, rewarding, and compensating young people during their formative years to demonstrate the desired behavior of the positive society that we want, together we would mold them into outstanding and brilliant beacons of true American democracy. This would also give us an economic cushion for uncertainties brought about by pandemics and other social ills.

America can do this by introducing our youth to mechanisms that make our nation work (voting, market economies) and incorporating them into these processes. Our children are our future, and we should incentivize, reward, and compensate them as such: *THE ANSWER*. We should design and build our future using an internal "junior" economy solely for youth participation, which could be treated like a separate sort of commonwealth that functions within our traditional economy that would give financial markets an internal boost. So here is A\WAY forward—A\WAY we can build the future, step into it, and transport our nation into the Great Beyond.

The "Teen New Deal" + Online Youth Market = "T.H.E. A.N.S.W.E.R."
(To Heal Everyone: A New Society With Education Rewards)

SUMMARY

All primary and secondary schools nationwide should have student government associations where students participate in a political process with student campaigns, elections, and voting. These schools would have their own separate youth voting bloc for student-related activities, as well as an internal market economy in which students earn funds to purchase goods and services within that market. Academic performance, social responsibility, and ethical behavior would be incentivized, rewarded, and compensated on a consistent basis using student licenses. When students transition to the traditional adult market, they will be better equipped to handle political and economic undertakings, contributing to a healthier and more stable outlook for society.

THE "TEEN NEW DEAL"

The Teen New Deal is A\WAY to transform society through educational reform by offering young Americans their own school-based market economy with jobs and wages via nationwide student government associations, a separate "youth currency" with parental access to student earnings, and an introductory vote. Being a student at school would be considered a legitimate occupation, and their earnings would be based on academic performance, social responsibility, and ethical behavior, which would be incentivized, rewarded, and compensated to reduce the severity and reoccurrence of behavior associated with inequity and injustice. Students would be consistently reminded of the ideal purpose of this Great American Experiment of a multi-ethnic mecca.

An introductory vote would mean that student votes would not have the exact weight of a voter in the traditional electorate of people 18 years of age and older. Their votes would only impact student affairs at the school level and may include an opposing or accompanying parental vote.

The Teen New Deal takes into consideration precedents that have already been set and simply expands upon them, namely youth labor and school-based student government associations. Teen labor is already in effect in major cities across America in the form of Summer Youth Employment Programs, some of which extend summer employment into autumn. The Teen New Deal seeks to extend youth employment all year round.

Many schools throughout the country operate student government associations or student councils. The National Student Council in Reston, Virginia, specializes in this work. The Teen New Deal suggests that student government associations be mandated in all schools nationwide for youth to practice voting on predetermined issues.

ONLINE YOUTH MARKET

An online youth marketplace/education exchange would be an organization in each state where primary and secondary students, along with their parents, purchase educational resources and supplies. The students would earn rewards and compensation based on school criteria, including social responsibility, ethical behavior, academic performance, attendance, student government association membership, dress code, volunteering, extracurricular activities, and contests/promotions.

Parents would be able to supervise student financial decisions with certain restrictions. For example, parents of elementary school children could have access to most of their child's earnings, perhaps 75–95 percent. As the students get older, parental access to student earnings decreases. In middle school, parents may have access to 60 percent of student earnings. Then, in each year of high school, parental access would decrease: perhaps 50 percent during freshman year; 40 percent in sophomore year; 30 percent in junior year; and 20 percent in senior year.

There would be private and public collaboration on curriculum and implementation. While corporations and other businesses would provide more effective and efficient operation of schools and the funds for student earnings, potentially with a digital currency or cryptocurrency, the federal government and parent advocacy groups would provide oversight.

THE ANSWER
To Heal Everyone: A New Society With Educational Rewards

America would duplicate the traditional adult market at the student level, allowing youth to "work" at school and have an introductory vote via their student government associations. Corporations and other businesses would recycle some of their profits into funds for student earnings. The federal government would create online youth marketplaces/education exchanges where students would redeem their earnings for academic performance, social responsibility, and ethical behavior.

Additionally, corporations and other businesses would sponsor and manage schools or school districts and fund student earnings with an alternative currency. Meanwhile, the federal government would provide oversight of fund management, including meaningful, transformative, and specific curriculum development in alignment with *THE ANSWER*.

Online youth marketplaces/education exchanges would operate from within, as an internal market, boosting traditional economic growth. As youth graduate from the student market into the traditional market, they will bring economic value and increased levels of academic performance, social responsibility, and ethical behavior. Federal, state, or local governments would tax students, contributing to their retirement pensions at an earlier age, which would further assist in sustaining the Social Security system.

The ultimate solution to reinvigorate the American economy and repair social inequities and injustices would be a society that incentivizes, rewards, and compensates people for demonstrating desired performances, responsibilities, and behavior. This would begin with youth in school and continue into adulthood. At a certain grade level, young Americans would be officially licensed as "students" for academic, social, and behavior work in the junior economy. Young people would practice the election process with an introductory vote to prepare for a lifetime of civic duty in which all Americans are rewarded to get along harmoniously.

Promotion from grade to grade would be rewarded in the youth market just as it would be in the traditional market. As certain standards and benchmarks are met, students would earn rewards and compensation. From childhood to adulthood, the federal government, corporations, and other businesses would continue an incentive-based approach to civics, offering compensation/wages with built-in incentives/rewards for Americans to succeed.

Socially, we would more effectively instill a moral compass within society by incentivizing, rewarding, and compensating our youth as they matriculate through school. Young adults would gain earlier financial literacy and independence. They could apply their earnings to future expenses including college and, more importantly, an earlier retirement.

Internationally, children around the world could expand their own nation's economy by participating in global youth marketplaces. Adults already out of school at the inception of the program would be offered rewards by their employer, federal, state, or local government for demonstrating desired responsibilities and behavior.

The social ills, inequities, and injustices that we seek to erase currently manifest in society as unfair personal exchanges between the government and civilians, namely systematic "racism," the skin-color syndrome; police brutality; and socioeconomic disparities. The government seeks to be more effective by limiting the nature of personal contact with Americans, but the drawback of this approach is a supposedly blind government that treats individuals, and even whole groups, as numbers instead of people.

Corporations and other businesses, on the other hand, excel past effectiveness through to efficiency when addressing concerns of the public. By capitalizing on the personal, emotional, and cultural needs of their employees, customers, clients, and communities, these corporations and other businesses are more likely to achieve professional harmony.

For government to achieve the success of corporations, entities in which almost everyone abides harmoniously, it must do as corporations and other businesses do and incentivize, reward, and compensate its populace, beginning with the youth. We should reward young people with more and better education and compensate them for adopting and demonstrating moral excellence that we have incentivized. This way we would produce a positive shift in civil exchanges between government officials and the American people.

Eventually, the youth who grow up to be police officers, politicians, and other officials who are educated using a more corporate approach would display a government that is more concerned with the personal well-being of the American people and the overall health of society. **_T.H.E. A.N.S.W.E.R. To Heal Everyone:_** To make America a truly sound democracy wherein natural Americans and immigrants alike feel secure and confident in the full implementation of our constitution and laws. **A New Society:** A new way for us to participate and interact with government and each other MUST be formed. This would include the federal, state, and local governments; corporations and other businesses; community, civic, and religious/ spiritual organizations; and each of us educating, incentivizing, and rewarding people of all ages and backgrounds to engage in lifelong learning and work. **With Educational Rewards:** Americans would fulfill National Identification (ID) requirements and contribute to their Social Security beginning in primary school by using their academic performance, social responsibility, and ethical behavior rewards and compensation. Upon finishing high school or college, Americans would maintain their National ID with a score or points similar to a credit score by adhering to a moral code consisting of continuous exchanges with government with guidance, incentives, rewards, compensation, and community support.

12 STEPS FOR A TEEN NEW DEAL

Government Legislation and Passage of Bills, Laws, Acts & Other Official Documents, and the Coordination Between the IRS, Social Security Administration & U.S. Department of Education

The U.S. Government would need to amend or update the Fair Labor Standards Act of 1938 which forbids labor of persons under the age of 16.

The IRS and Social Security Administration will need to adopt new practices to accommodate an enlarged labor pool due to students being added to the workforce. They will be tax-paying citizens and some of their earnings will be funneled into pension accounts for retirement giving the Social Security system the boost that it needs. Because youth would be entering the workforce sooner, they could be eligible for an earlier retirement age. Coordination with the U.S. Department of Education would be necessary to determine how students would be compensated and rewarded at school for academic and moral labor.

Monetary Reform/Government Adoption and Issuance of New Youth Currency, Digital/Crypto Currency

Two options to fund student rewards/compensation are presented here:

A. (Recommended) The federal government could offer corporations and other businesses incentives to pay student earnings directly out of corporate profits by donating into a fund which is converted into "youth" currency.

B. The federal government could divert a portion of current education budget into a fund and convert into "youth" currency to pay student wages.

In either case, the government may gain the most economic benefit by issuing student earnings via digital currency or cryptocurrency (i.e., electronic money, Bitcoin, Coinbase) using a secure form of information communication technology called blockchain. Blockchain is a rapidly growing and popular form of financial market offering advanced security and can be described as closed-circuit internet for select participants.

The proponents of these new digital currency and cryptocurrency forms are forecasting an exponential increase in transactions done with these currencies. However, to solidify legitimacy and establish a viable financial market, there must be a demand by one or more industries with enough consumers or participants to effectuate hundreds of millions, even billions of transactions. With 50 million American youth working in schools and more than a billion more youth around the globe, this would be the perfect time to bring digital currency and cryptocurrency to the masses. The global youth population would be an invaluable addition to the economy, offering substantial opportunities for market growth and investments.

The federal government would establish equal wages digitally for all students, depending on state, to avoid inequity. Another alternative would be to switch the traditional economy to digital currency or cryptocurrency and have the online youth marketplace/ education exchange function with cash. As youth transition into the adult economy, they would bring added value when their "youth" currency converts back to the traditional American dollar.

Design and Build an Online Youth Market and/or "Education Exchanges" for Each State

Each state could be responsible for their own online youth marketplace/education exchange after a national youth currency has been adopted. Alternatively, there could be one exchange under the purvey of the federal government in which students could access their respective state exchange. Students and parents would create user accounts linked to the school, their National ID, Social Security numbers, and a digital/crypto bank account/wallet, a sub-account listed under the parent's bank account. Students and parents would be able to access their specific profile and account information, including grades, citizenship records, earnings, deductions, and purchase history.

The online youth marketplace/education exchange would be available year-round for students to purchase items and services associated with school (books, uniforms, school lunches, field trips, classes). The exchange could also have a link to the school calendar so that students would know what upcoming expenses for which to plan. There would also be promotions and service announcements to alert students and parents about various educational programs and services, job opportunities, available rewards, wage tables, and associated apps.

During the enrollment stage, (birth to 7 years old for example), students would only earn funds and would not be eligible for purchases until they reach a designated level (age 8). During that advanced stage, students would then be allowed to make purchases using funds earned in the enrollment stage. Every year thereafter, students and parents would make purchases via the online youth marketplace/education exchange with incentives, rewards, and compensation earned in the previous school year or enrollment stage. If students or parents desire or need to access funds earned in the current year, a penalty could be assessed.

Development of Incentive-Based Rewards Curriculum & Culture for Students & Adults & the Establishment of the Great American Experiment curriculum & a Moral Code Commitment

The daily lesson plans students engage in would have built-in opportunities for teachers to distribute random and regular incentives, rewards, and compensation. To ensure that society, students, and adults acknowledge their social and civic responsibilities as part of the Great American Experiment, there would be incentives in place for positive reinforcement. Youth could earn rewards and compensation to meet traditional benchmarks in school along with new ones. Schools could offer students an annual incentive upon promotion to the next grade level, and students could also receive rewards for avoiding social ills, e.g., delaying parenthood until a certain age, saying no to drugs, enrolling in approved classes or programs that teach responsible drug use, and nurturing their health.

To ensure the ongoing transformation of American society,

students would be continually educated about the factual history of our nation to discourage repetitive future conflict. A socially conscious curriculum, combined with continuous rewards is necessary to develop ongoing social awareness and further change. There would be frequent opportunities to earn rewards and reinforce a moral code of excellence, which could take many forms such as public and electronic acknowledgements, moral code contracts, and other formal commitments.

Certification of Principals, Teachers, Staff, Student Government Officials

Mandated training and education would be required to certify that all principals, teachers, staff, and student government association members are skilled to distribute rewards and wages associated with the new incentive-based curriculum. Teachers may have user accounts for the online youth marketplace/education exchange.

Nationwide Student Government Associations

The federal government would operate a duplicate or mock version of government at the youth level and all students would be issued youth voting rights linked to their National ID. Students would participate in annual school- based campaigns and elections and would decide solutions based on challenges designed for them to overcome. Their vote would not have the same weight as the adult vote in the traditional electorate and may solely apply to school issues and affairs. Student government association members would receive a stipend or reward for their service. Millions of jobs would be created for adults to guide and monitor students through the process of operating a junior government and economy.

National I.D. Requirements and Certification

All students would have a student National ID. The privilege of real freedom and true democracy are incredible responsibilities to uphold and maintain as part of the Great American Experiment. *THE ANSWER* proposed would require people to certify their ability to maintain that privilege of being a free American with annual requirements to renew National ID based on a score or points earned for adherence to laws and moral codes. People with a higher score or more points on their license would earn more rewards and compensation. People with deductions would be denied certain opportunities and, if their score or points fall below a predetermined level, more education would be provided.

Creation of Student Jobs and Workforce Database & Wage Structure with Parental Access to Earnings

Being a "student" would be a legitimate occupation with roles, responsibilities, and associated wages or rewards for certain school-based activities. The student workforce database would list all student jobs, activities, wages, and rewards that accompany them. Parents would have access to student earnings until the student graduates from high school. Parental access to student earnings would be based on student age/grade and come with certain restrictions.

As the youth gets older, parental access to student earnings would minimize. For example, parents of elementary school children would have access to most of their child's earnings, perhaps 75–95 percent. As the student gets older, parental access to the earnings decreases. In middle school, parents may have access to 60 percent of student earnings. Then, in each year of high school, parental access decreases each year: freshman-year parents may have access to 50 percent; sophomore-year parental access may decrease to 40 percent; 30 percent in junior year; and 20 percent during senior year.

The portion of funds that the student retains are for personal use only on the online youth marketplace/education exchange. Students can make purchases, invest, transfer, and donate. They would also be rewarded and compensated to maintain a certain balance or to make smart spending decisions.

Development of Tax Incentives/Rewards for Parents

To assure more parent involvement in the academic life of children there could be additional tax incentives offered through the Teen New Deal. Depending on the earnings/rewards of their children their taxable income could be offset. There could also be other opportunities/rewards offered at the online youth market for parents to take advantage of.

Development of Tax Incentives for Corporations and Other Businesses

To ensure adequate funding of online youth marketplaces/education exchanges in every state, there could be additional tax incentives, such as tax credits and abatements, offered to corporations and other businesses that donate to a national fund or sponsor their local schools or school districts.

Small business opportunities would be created for previously marginalized communities to produce the goods and services consumed by the youth market.

Informing the Public About the Teen New Deal, National ID Requirements, Additional Jobs in the Adult Workforce, and Government Legislation to Build & Support the Online Youth Marketplace/Education Exchange

An ongoing national campaign (online, tv, radio, print) would be needed to inform the public about the Teen New Deal, how it will transform society and create tremendous job growth, and what citizens can do to participate and take advantage of *THE ANSWER*—America's ideal opportunity for redemption. At the school level, principals, teachers, and student government association members would educate the student population about how the online youth marketplace/education exchange operates.

For true democracy in a modern, technology-fueled era, citizens should be required and rewarded to fulfill National ID requirements. There should be multiple options for citizens to demonstrate civic participation. The federal government could offer incentives for civil service in a role like teacher, sanitation worker, postal employee, firefighter, police officer, or military personnel; or perhaps offer citizens random rewards for various patriotic efforts such as volunteering, donating services/goods, and other positive activities.

Millions of jobs will be available in the adult workforce to build and staff an online youth marketplace/education exchange in every state and support the junior economy.

Launch

Let Americans Unite Nationwide Coordinated Healing (**LAUNCH**) is a strategic movement to maintain momentum. **Let Americans Unite:** We The People must use the power of government legislation for ourselves, to strengthen our American institutions by folding our youth into the economic fabric of our nation and creating a separate but guided youth market. **Nationwide:** Because America is a nation of immigrants by design—open to all—and that all who come here represent all the tribes, nations, cultures, ethnicities, and human beings of our beloved Earth, then when we speak of "Americans" healing "nationwide," we are really speaking of all humans healing globally and, ideally, in a coordinated manner. **Coordinated Healing:** Understanding the evolution of human technology into social media offers insight into the pros and cons associated with the entire world population communicating more closely. To properly heal humanity and traditional adult markets from within, we must responsibly build and maintain the youth markets to ensure the successful growth and development of youth into adults able to thrive and communicate in an extremely advanced technological era, completely different from the upbringing of previous generations.

Once government legislation has been approved; online infrastructure has been designed; currency and exchange rates have been adopted; and the nation is educated about, and prepared for, the Teen New Deal and associated programs, America can march forward to a much smarter and brighter future.

As flawed as our current system may be, it has gotten our nation to this point and serves as the fuel that we need to propel us even beyond the future that we desire. Change is inevitable and necessary. If America continues using it, the current system will become obsolete and destroy any dreams of the America that the founders may have envisioned.

THE ANSWER will enable us to step further A\ WAY from our past, change our present, and propel ourselves beyond the future by...

CHAPTER

A\WAY (BEYOND)

...adding the youth populace to the American economy, giving them an introductory vote, and incentivizing, rewarding, and compensating them to transform society through their academic and moral labor. As the initial implementation of Social Security helped propel Americans out of the Great Depression, adding youth to the system now would serve as the "Great Transition" into the beyond. Our entire nation focused on one common goal—sewing young people into the economic fabric of America—would nurture, heal, and unite society.

Youth participation in student government associations would equate to future leaders who are better groomed to handle the complex affairs of a diverse global community. As adults guide the youth through the social ills, inequities, and injustices passed onto their youth market, the adult market would lead by example, incentivizing, rewarding, and compensating the youth along the way. The traditional adult market may incorporate solutions that youth develop into their market, and vice versa. Americans would heal ourselves, our economies, and our nation internally.

Future youth who have grown through the Great Transition would become outstanding and brilliant beacons of true American democracy. With the potential to drive social, government, and global reform beyond the current generation, Americans would experience a positive social and economic shift across multiple reform areas, including the following and beyond:

BEYOND BLACK & WHITE
(AMERICAN CULTURAL & ETHNIC BACKGROUNDS)
With Americans that grew up as students who were incentivized, rewarded, and compensated to do the right thing with an introductory right to vote...

In the beyond, Americans are compensated and rewarded to recognize the value of different perspectives and to embrace people of all cultural and ethnic backgrounds. Traditions include new and ongoing exchanges for people to acknowledge the contributions of one another. To achieve and maintain true cultural and ethnic harmony, there must be genuine and mutual respect among the descendants of the three groups central to our nation's origin: (1) the indigenous or Aboriginal/Native "American" tribes and their descendants; (2) the European immigrants and their immediate descendants; and (3) the African "slaves" and their descendants.

The "black" and "white" skin-color labels of the past are deemed as insufficient and as catalysts of oppressive division, hatred, and xenophobia in a world where human beings of all cultures and ethnicities are supposed to be one race of people. The "black" and "white" people of America were the only two ethnic groups on Earth identified by the only two colors that are considered opposites. People recognize that this was oppositional in nature and would keep Americans at odds with one another if not changed.

New identifiers are adopted for each group, reflective of their contribution to our nation—not their skin color. Legislation is passed so that the Social Security Administration, U.S. Census Bureau, and other governmental organizations can amend identifying documents and applications. Indigenous or Aboriginal/Native American tribes and their descendants are known as "Indie-American," "indie" being short for "indigenous" and "independent," as they were the first independent societies known to occupy this land. "White"/European immigrants and their descendants have assumed the moniker "Tru-American," evidencing the idea of a democratic republic as the brainchild of a people fleeing economic oppression and classism by the nobility of Europe. "Black"/African slaves and their descendants, having been subjected to an even harsher marginalization than their oppressors previously faced in their own homeland, have taken on the designation "Neo/Nu American," demonstrating solidarity and trust between all three counterparts. Immigrants to America of all other nationalities became affectionately known as "Immi-American," a nod to a televised entertainment industry awards program (Emmy Awards), as immigrants who won citizenship status in America.

To maintain this trust and solidarity, Americans from all four groups continuously and meaningfully acknowledge each group's contribution to history by participating in a national recognition ceremony during annual Fourth of July festivities. The nation adopts the following four guiding notions of American cultural/ethnic harmony because they combine to form a theme involving acceptance of one another:

(1) **The Vision of America**, a land for all peoples united in democracy, can be attributed to the economic oppression and mental fortitude of European immigrants and their immediate descendants, and the foresight with which they envisioned our nation, so this honor rests with them, now Tru Americans.

(2) **The Building of America** and the financial rewards reaped by Tru Americans from harvesting its resources can be attributed to the slave labor and mental fortitude of Africans and their immediate descendants, and the grace with which they accepted inhumane transgressions for centuries, so this honor rests with them, now Neo/Nu-Americans.

(3) **The Permission of the American Dream** to manifest was given by people of "color" coexisting in the land long before the birth of the nation, and can be attributed to the willingness of Indigenous/Native American tribes to sacrifice financial gain and their ancestral right to the earth in or-

der that the peoples of the world could form a more perfect union, so this honor rests with them, now Indie-Americans.

(4) **The Continuance of America** to exist as a land of opportunity for all peoples around the world, can be attributed to immigrants who give themselves permission to leave their original homelands, chase their own dreams and visions, and try to make them a reality in America, so this honor rests with them, now Immi-Americans.

During the ceremony Neo/Nu-, Tru-, and Immi-Americans join to honor Indie-Americans; Indie-, Tru-, and Immi-Americans join to honor Neo/Nu Americans; Indie-, Neo/Nu-, and Immi-Americans join to honor Tru Americans; and Indie-, Neo/Nu-, and Tru Americans join to honor Immi Americans.

In the beyond, Americans recognize that in the past, most citizens could only identify one month that specifically celebrates the cultural and ethnic contributions and achievements of any one group, e.g., February as "'Black' History Month." Student government association members and other student activists create a successful movement to have each month nationally recognized as honoring a different group of Americans. The U.S. Secretary of Education issues a national mandate for all public schools to focus each month on the following cultures, ethnicities, and groups:

U.S. HERITAGE MONTHS	
January Tru-American History Month	**July** Men's History Month
February Neo/Nu-American History Month	**August** Civil Servants' History Month
March Indie-American History Month	**September** Disabled History Month
April Immi-American History Month	**October** Military/Veteran's History Month
May Women's History Month	**November** World History Month
June LGBTQ History Month	**December** Religious/Spiritual History Month

America incentivizes, rewards, and compensates people to develop more cross cultural/ethnic relationships, and the skin-color syndrome, "racism," and hatred begin to diminish. Cultural/ethnic traditions include new and ongoing exchanges for people to recognize and acknowledge the contributions of one another.

In New York City, for example, there were many segregated parades celebrating individual cultures and ethnicities (St. Patrick's Day Parade, Caribbean-American Day Parade, Korean Day Parade, and several others). New Yorkers create a new parade in the beyond, the Cross-Cultural/Ethnicities Bridge Day Parade. It consists of various cultures and ethnicities together as one, parading across one or more of New York City's bridges as a reminder to embrace acceptance and bridge the gaps across cultural, ethnic, and other boundaries. *(See Beyond Reparations.)*

BEYOND ECONOMICS
With Americans that grew up as students who were incentivized, rewarded, and compensated to do the right thing with an introductory right to vote...

In the beyond, students will be rewarded to compete for earnings and invest inside a smaller, "Junior" economy with a "youth" currency inside an online youth market/education exchange. There will be youth versions of the Dow Jones, Nasdaq, and S&P and youth will be taught how to invest in these exchanges. Upon transitioning to the larger adult market, their portfolio earnings will take on a larger value and expand the economy.

Through the passing of groundbreaking immigration reform acts, particularly **ALIENS**, **SHIFT**, and Reverse-Immigration, the economy sees a major financial boost through new migratory patterns and the real-estate markets. "Black" and "brown" (Nu/Neo and Indie-American) communities experience major wealth building with business opportunities extending from the creation of the online youth marketplace/educational exchange. *(See Beyond Immigration, Beyond Reparations,)*

BEYOND EDUCATION
With Americans that grew up as students who were incentivized, rewarded, and compensated to do the right thing with an introductory right to vote...

In the beyond, American students compete for rewards in both academics and citizenship. Schools reward students regularly and frequently for their intellectual and moral prowess, and students mature earlier with incentive-based curriculums focused heavily on social issues, such as "racism," sexism, ageism, and other "ism's."

With emphasis on the Great American Experiment, a federally mandated curriculum and collaboration between the U.S. Departments of Justice and Education, educators in the beyond focus on incentivizing, rewarding, and compensating students to learn accurate history about the mission of America to spread democratic ideals and education globally. Furthermore, "white" (Tru-American) xenophobes are reminded that their ancestors had also been oppressed and marginalized in Europe in the past, which was the reason for their immigration to America. To marginalize "black" and "brown" (Nu/Neo-American) people was repeating the history of oppression that their own ancestors had escaped from other "white" people. It is also theorized among intellectuals that harmony among the so-called "races" is essential for the whole human race to continue its advance from tribal, to global, to cosmic thinking.

Classes and instruction in the beyond are more closely tied to a person's actual life, and incentives/rewards can be attached to one's National ID. For example, students may earn more credits in math class for maintaining a certain savings account balance or more credit in health class for maintaining their health. Students reach financial literacy sooner, thus creating a populace better able to handle debts. While the youth develop solutions for financial affairs in the youth market, the adults guiding them develop solutions for the adult market, and vice versa. The entire educational field shifts as students and other eligible participants are rewarded to know and do better.

American students look upon actual history through the lens of evolution and science. They understand that humanity as a species has flowered upon planet Earth just like birds, bees, vegetation, and all other organic matter. Our presence is part of the biological contribution to the environment. Americans look upon past social tension and conflict as part of a necessary process that humans had to endure as part of our sprouting into resilient beings who thrive and flourish amidst crises.

To encourage youth participation in student government associations and to make social media and entertainment more age appropriate, internet and television programming for students are consolidated by the U.S. Department of Education with the formation of **Y**outh Education/**E**ntertainment **T**elenet (**YEET**), a national closed-circuit internet/television network for schools. Several channels compete on YEET for the youth education/entertainment audience, the most popular being **SPACEBOOK**. The organization's moniker is famously known in the beyond as an acronym that boldly demonstrates their mission to curating high quality age-appropriate content – **S**uitable **P**resently **A**ppropriate **C**ommunication **E**nforcement **B**anning **O**bviously **O**bscene **K**nowledge. Americans in the beyond also determine, that going forward, after providing citizens with traditional education for the first two decades of life, providing incentives and rewards for ongoing educational support during the remainder of adult life is the most responsible path. What was known as "television" in the past, has transitioned into a network for adult, age-based and incentivized programming, the **G**raduate **E**ducation **T**elenet (**GET**).

(See Beyond Environment, Beyond Healthcare, Beyond "Nigger," Beyond Religion/Spirituality, Beyond Social Security, Beyond Substance Abuse.)

BEYOND ENVIRONMENT
With Americans that grew up as students who were incentivized, rewarded, and compensated to do the right thing with an introductory right to vote...

In the beyond, scientists and educators believe that the term "climate change" is insufficient and they suggest an acronym that more accurately acknowledges how humans impact the climate: **HICCUP**, **H**uman **I**mpact **C**limate **C**hange **U**rgently **P**rioritized. Americans are taught, incentivized, and rewarded to understand science and believe that the climate on Earth changes over long periods of time. They also believe that human activities on our planet, such as industrialization, deforestation, pollution, and other activities, rapidly change the climate and, if left unchecked, would be extremely detrimental to the long-term survival of our species. In the beyond, people are taught that, because an individual human has a limited lifespan, then the collective human existence on earth may be some kind of countdown as opposed to an unlimited period of time that we may have our way with.

Scientists understand, in the larger context of our solar system and universe/multiverse, that human beings producing technology is like birds and bees participating in the pollination process of plants and flowers. Just as those small creatures can contribute to large-scale changes across the planet, scientists realize the purpose of human technology on Earth may be to support a larger cosmic event in which the climate of several planets may change dramatically, swiftly, and perhaps simultaneously.

In the beyond, students and other Americans, as well as entire communities, cities, and states are rewarded for their positive contributions to renewable energy and conservation efforts. For example, the residents of cities or states who reduce their carbon footprint more in any given year are eligible for lower taxes, increased compensation, or rewards from the federal government. *(See Beyond Education.)*

BEYOND EVOLUTION
With Americans that grew up as students who were incentivized, rewarded, and compensated to do the right thing with an introductory right to vote...

In the beyond, lessons have been learned after clearing another pandemic with the benefits of an online youth market. The majority of Americans recognize the significance of following the components of science—research, theories, facts, evidence, patterns and proof—which led to progress that benefits the whole society. Charles Darwin's theory of evolution is no longer disputed widely, and the portal is wide open to envision more progressive theories such as the **T**heory of **I**nterplanetary **E**volution (**TIE**), allowing broader discourse regarding the place and purpose of humanity and Earth in this Solar System/Universe/Multiverse and beyond.

TIE is an expansion of evolution, a prequel. It postulates that the planets in our Solar System grow and develop through a process of evolution exact in nature to that of human beings. In fact, TIE states in the beyond, planetary evolution is the reason for human evolution as both processes are tidally locked, so much so that human traits and characteristics are based on planetary traits as a model. The crux of the TIE argument: Our Solar System is a unit of time/space/energy functioning on the quantum scale of a larger reality that is our Universe; the nine, well-known planets are actually nine separate stages in the development of one planetary body of energy, birthed out of the Sun; the body of energy is "living" out a journey, according to an ordered sequence through the time/space unit, spiraling out to the edge of time/space at the Solar System's edge, where the body of energy (planet) appears to decompose and refuel the unit. This all happens to our "Solar System/Time-Space Unit" within a quantifiably short amount of time in the larger reality that surrounds us as the Universe. However, to our human minds functioning within and as a part of the Solar System, the time appears to us on a much larger scale, billions of years, infinitely even. *(See Beyond Education.)*

BEYOND GUNS
With Americans that grew up as students who were incentivized, rewarded, and compensated to do the right thing with an introductory right to vote...

In the beyond, students and other Americans realize that guns and other violent weapons are obsolete, false forms of security. At the inception of our nation, guns were a new technology that made people feel safe and secure in a lawless land. Current 911 and other security systems did not exist, so it made sense hundreds of years ago to include guns as a right for new Americans. People in the beyond know that if the United States of America was formed in a more technologically advanced era, internet access and healthcare would be a guaranteed right for citizens—not guns—and that gun advocacy was a political ploy in the past (our present) to promote gun violence in underserved communities.

Americans are incentivized in the beyond to own fewer guns and participate in more lawful, morally upright behavior. Youth move into society as adults who have been incentivized, rewarded, and compensated to uphold certain values and ethics, and the need for guns and police has evolved.

Guns are repurposed for theatrical value, and ownership criteria are strictly enforced. Gun owners are required to store firearms at public storage facilities and checking them out requires preapproval based on need. For example, added security for domestic violence victims, residents in neighborhoods with elevated crime, or CHIP alerts. Guns and other weapons, such as explosive devices and missiles, are part of art exhibitions and installations at "war and violence" museums. "War" has become an elevated version of the "Cold War," a war of ideas from the past. Winners of battles may be determined by technological skill and demonstration of intellectual prowess using various humane techniques, including **T**actical **Re**sponse **I**nitiated **V**ia Intellectual **A**ttack (**TRIVIA**) and **ATHLETICS**, an agreement between warring nations/factions in the beyond to solve conflict using sports – **A**lternative **T**o **H**ateful **L**ife **E**xecutions **T**hrough **I**nternationally **C**oordinated **S**ports. *(See Beyond Prison.)*

BEYOND HEALTHCARE
With Americans that grew up as students who were incentivized, rewarded, and compensated to do the right thing with an introductory right to vote...

In the beyond, students and other Americans are rewarded from their youth to meet certain health standards like avoiding tooth cavities or sexually transmitted diseases. With the aid of technology, Americans earn points on their National ID for being more health conscious. With a longer and better quality of life, people are more proactive about taking preventive health measures, and the government and medical community are less burdened with the woes of an ailing society. *(See Beyond Education.)*

BEYOND HOMELESSNESS
With Americans that grew up as students who were incentivized, rewarded, and compensated to do the right thing with an introductory right to vote...

Homelessness is a thing of the past due to the establishment of **HEAT**, **H**omeless **E**ducation **A**id **T**askforce. Local institutes solely for people on the verge of, or mired in homelessness are operating nationwide for individuals and families to enroll, with tuition and boarding expenses covered. Classes and workshops are tailored toward mental health and artistic expression. Unlike traditional colleges and universities, there are expanded graduation options, including continued education at a traditional 4-year institute; offers of employment, such as visiting lecturer or artist-in-residence at a HEAT establishment; or, perhaps, transfer to a mental institution if necessary. HEAT establishments are considered a viable option for immigrants as well as newly released inmates. *(See Beyond Immigration, Beyond Prison.)*

BEYOND IMMIGRATION
With Americans that grew up as students who were incentivized, rewarded, and compensated to do the right thing with an introductory right to vote...

In the beyond, students and other Americans are rewarded from their youth to value diversity and appreciate the fact that America is a nation of immigrants by design. Leaders acknowledge that our true strength rests in the embrace of all cultures and ethnicities. America is the conduit for democracy that it should be, not just a destination. Immigrants earn their way into our country by paying the debt of current citizens via proposed legislation known as **ALIENS** (**A**lways **L**et **I**mmigrants **E**nter **N**ation **S**ecurely).

When an immigrant wants to become a citizen of the United States, in addition to passing U.S. Citizenship exams, they gain online or on-site employment with an American corporation or other sponsor from a list of approved businesses. They can also gain housing with a HEAT institute. The sponsoring organization pays this "pre citizen" using a discounted digital currency or cryptocurrency, a portion of which goes to the worker, and a portion is credited to the IRS debt of an existing American citizen. Immigrants gain full citizenship when the debt of an existing citizen, or portion thereof, is paid through this modern reboot of indentured servitude. The existing citizen gets a higher tax score; the sponsoring organization receives discounted labor; and an immigrant securely gains U.S. citizenship and advances to the traditional adult market with added value.

Immigrants also have increased paths to U.S. citizenship through SHIFT and "Reverse-Immigration," legislation incentivizing Americans to make room for immigrants by moving to Canada,

Great Britain, or Australia. *(See Beyond Economics, Beyond Homelessness, Beyond Veiled "White" Supremacy.)*

BEYOND MALE MEMORIALS & MONUMENTS
With Americans that grew up as students who were incentivized, rewarded, and compensated to do the right thing with an introductory right to vote...

In the beyond, students and other Americans recognize that, in the past, there had been an under-representation of women in national memorials and monuments. Americans decide to mint all primary U.S. coins with the faces of women.

Because there were no women memorialized on the National Mall in the District of Columbia, our nation's capital, Americans in the beyond erect a new monument to honor female Supreme Court Justices. Considered a monument-in-progress, this memorial is to be continually updated as new female justices are appointed to the bench. Called the Hall of Justice, the monument features elegant and oversized statues of the only five female Supreme Court Justices out of 115 total that had ever been appointed since the Supreme Court was established in 1789:

(1) Sandra Day O'Connor;

(2) Ruth Bader Ginsburg;

(3) Sonia Sotomayor;

(4) Elena Kagan; and

(5) Amy Coney Barrett,

with four open spaces reserved for future female Supreme Court Justices. There are nine seats on the Supreme Court bench.

The Hall of Justice is built at the opposite end of the National Mall as an anchor to the Lincoln Memorial. This site is the former location of a professional sports arena for an unnamed team that previously used a racial slur to identify itself.

In the beyond, to honor American presidents dedicated to the push for increased diversity and acceptance, former President Joseph Biden is added to Mount Rushmore. Biden is recognized for the diversity of presidential and vice-presidential candidates that he had endorsed. Former President Barack Obama replaces former President Abraham Lincoln on the $5 bill as a salute to Lincoln's legacy of the Emancipation Proclamation.

Inspired by the national dialogue surrounding increased memorials recognizing women and non-"white" (non-Tru-American) males, a coalition of female, "black," and "brown" (Nu/Neo- and Indie-American) lawmakers, and their allies, introduce, pass, and enact affirmative action legislation for the U.S. presidency. This Act is called **S**top **H**olding **A**ll **R**esources **E**ternally (**SHARE**). If there has been a "white" (Tru-American) male president for three consecutive terms, all parties must only nominate alternative candidates.

BEYOND NIGGER
With Americans that grew up as students who were incentivized, rewarded, and compensated to do the right thing with an introductory right to vote...

In the beyond, students and other Americans recognize that the word "nigger" had been weaponized in the past to mentally and psychologically assault Africans who were captured and forced into slave labor. The descendants of slave owners and other racist xenophobes continued to perpetuate that assault on Africans and their descendants. "Nigger" was adopted by Africans and their descendants as a form of self-defense, self preservation, and even self love. While the "white" (Tru-American) xenophobes used "nigger" with hatred and hostility, "black" (Nu/Neo-American) people began using it toward one another in both hostile and nonhostile manners, often indicating a love for one another. One drawback of this unexpected development was that "black" people had conditioned themselves into continued use of "nigger," which is a point-blank weapon formed against them. This led to a sense of accomplishment for racist "white" xenophobes and encouraged those in political and leadership positions to maintain a government rife with systemic racism.

To combat damage done by use of the word, Americans in the beyond have completely contextualized "nigger" through educational reform and social media. To heal our nation, schools and community organizations implement holistic and socially conscious classes/workshops designed to wean people from continued use of "nigger." The process or course is known as "**N**igger" **De**compression and **De**programming (**InDeep**). Americans are taught to remove "nigger" from their vocabulary just like one pulls a knife from a stab wound so that its use may be studied and analyzed as a weapon after a crime. Previously abbreviated the "N-word," psychologists and other authorities have deemed that term too passive an approach to healing. They suggest that, to fully diminish the harm associated with "nigger," it must be used point-blank in educational settings only.

Another similar curriculum course is enacted in the beyond to combat verbal violence, **SLUR**, or **S**candalous **L**anguage **U**sed **Re**sponsibly. Participants take courses on decent and offensive language and explore how words are used in different situational experiences. For instance, the course "Slurs 101" explores three social settings to shed light on how words deemed to be slurs can also be decent, in a healthy manner: a Physical Education classroom; a tense employment confrontation; a sexual encounter. In the PE class youth are taught using the anatomical labels *vagina* and *penis* and may also reference the alternative, vulgar terms *pussy, cunt,* and *cock.* It would also be noted that variations of these terms, shouted during another social setting, a confrontation between coworkers, "*cunt!*" or "*dick!*" for example, could evoke a derogatory meaning without an actual sexual implication. However, the irony of our language and existence would be highlighted and explored further upon noting that derogatory language during sexual encounters is considered appropriate but using anatomical labels taught in PE classrooms is a non-traditional approach during sex.

At schools in the beyond, where the **SLUR** curriculum is taught, students may choose to pay a fine or have points assessed on their ID for use of derogatory language in certain social settings. An incentive/reward is given to students who avoid **SLUR** penalties. Other ethnic and cultural slurs (*retard, dyke, faggot, chink, cracker, spic, redskin, etc.*) are included in these courses to achieve healing for multiple communities.

BEYOND OLD GLORY
With Americans that grew up as students who were incentivized, rewarded, and compensated to do the right thing with an introductory right to vote...

In the beyond, students and other Americans understand that our nation is a continually evolving work in progress. This is evident when looking at the variations of the American flag. It began with 13 stars representing the original 13 colonies. Eventually, the stars increased to represent the 50 states that existed at that time. In the early 21st century when residents of our nation's capital tried to achieve statehood for the District of Columbia as the 51st state, independent artists had begun to create more inclusive versions of the American flag to symbolize the rich cultural and ethnic diversity at the heart of our nation. In the beyond, during Fourth of July festivities, Americans still honor artists that are inspired to design flags that symbolize moving past the systemic skin-color syndrome of "racism" and marginalization that had plagued the country. Many of the new flag variations include the color purple, which symbolizes royalty and is the combination of red and blue, the colors of the two previously dominant political parties in the United States of America. *(See Beyond Patriotism Versus Protest.)*

BEYOND PANDEMICS
With Americans that grew up as students who were incentivized, rewarded, and compensated to do the right thing with an introductory right to vote...

In the beyond, Americans use the online youth marketplace/education exchange to counter the disruptive effects of pandemics and other crises. With access to student earnings and investments, parents have additional financial resources should they become unemployed. Americans realize that, although they are rare, biological outbreaks are just as much a threat to humanity as economic depressions and nuclear war. As a result of past pandemics in the early and late 21st century, people have learned that biological outbreaks may be used as an advantage in warfare and even as a tool of economic and social oppression.

Looking back on the historic 2020 COVID-19 pandemic, citizens realize in the beyond, that officials never publicly warned what would happen if the public didn't wear masks and shut down public venues – breakdown of society due to an overwhelmed medical system. Strategists and analysts knew that providing misinformation and limited accurate information about biological outbreaks or minimizing their severity would increase mortality rates in targeted communities and have crippling economic effects. Some individuals allegedly acting as patriots were willing to be infected to intentionally infect others, believing access to superior healthcare would help them get away with it. Additionally, fear and disinformation could easily spread through the social media of the time and distract citizens from the truth: The majority of Americans had already been vaccinated several times in their youth as it was a routine and widespread practice for at least the previous half century!!

Because the youth market is built on a separate, secure digital network using blockchain technology in the beyond, and because science is highly regarded in the educational field, the online youth marketplace/education exchange is a trusted source for dissemination of reliable information, particularly during crises. The federal government mandates that the Emergency Broadcast System and the National Weather Service coordinate efficient and effective vaccine distributions via the adult and youth markets. *(See Beyond Education.)*

BEYOND PATRIOTISM VERSUS PROTESTS
With Americans that grew up as students who were incentivized, rewarded, and compensated to do the right thing with an introductory right to vote...

In the beyond, students and other Americans understand that the United States of America and its founding documents, the U.S. Declaration of Independence and the Constitution of the United States of America, are active forms of protest. Being born as an American citizen is being born as a protester, and becoming an American citizen is being born again, as a protester. In America, protesting is a form of patriotism.

People realize that, in the past, there had been conflict between Americans about the traditions followed during the observance of the National Anthem and the Pledge of Allegiance. This conflict stemmed from differences in opinion on how to express one's patriotism during those practices. To avoid future tension, Americans in the beyond restructure the observances with opportunities for citizens to express their patriotism, both protest and support. Before and after the anthem is to be sung or the pledge is to be recited, individuals wishing to express their patriotism, whether protest or support, in A\WAY that is peaceful are allowed to do so. Protesters may face away from the flag with their hands clasped behind them, take a knee, or hold a fist in the air while saying aloud their critique. Supporters may face the flag, hold their hand over their heart or salute and say aloud what they appreciate about America. *(See Beyond Old Glory.)*

BEYOND PRISON
With Americans that grew up as students who were incentivized, rewarded, and compensated to do the right thing with an introductory right to vote...

In the beyond, students and other Americans readily recognize that disparities in the prison population represent extreme inequity and injustice. The benefit of reward and compensation for conscientious moral service to society is too tempting to resist, and three possible options become apparent: (1) to dramatically increase the number of "white" (Tru American) prisoners; (2) to dramatically decrease the number of "black" and "brown" (Nu/Neo American) prisoners; or (3) to destroy the whole system and begin from scratch, making sure that the number of prisoners is relative to the entire general population. Americans in the beyond choose the latter. Proposed legislation known as **M.O.S.E.S.** (**M**ake **O**ver **S**ociety, **E**nding **S**entences) introduces potential solutions.

Americans recognize the historic presence of systemic "racism"—the skin-color syndrome—and gender bias, particularly in criminal justice, and they acknowledge that this led to the incarceration of innocent men, women, and children. Due to immeasurable disproportions in the number of imprisoned "black" and "brown" (Nu/Neo) men and women, as well as "white" (Tru American) women, versus the incarceration of "white" (Tru American) men specifically, Americans determined that maintaining this extremely xenophobic and sexist penal system is the personification of inequity and injustice and must be transformed, even abolished.

To establish precise innocence of those wrongfully imprisoned is very time consuming by design and adds even more insult and injury to those innocent victims who were stripped of their inalienable human rights and their lives. To combat future disparities in incarceration the prison population is managed based on the general population. For example, if "white" (Tru-American) men are 25 percent of the general American population they are 25 percent of the prison population. If incarceration rates become disproportionate, members of the communities affected receive increased rewards/compensations, while members of nonsuffering communities receive decreased rewards/compensations.

CHIP (**C**riminal **H**ints **I**n **P**roximity) is a program developed to wipe the slate of criminal "justice" clean. Over the course of several years, the federal government orders the strategically timed release of all prisoners into pre-approved custodies using Global Positioning System (GPS) tracking and body camera (bodycam) technologies. Many former prisoners enroll into HEAT establishments and are incentivized and rewarded to maintain morally upright behavior in a new America. Any recent crimes they are suspected of are confirmed with GPS monitoring and bodycam evidence. When former prisoners are in the vicinity, people receive proximity alerts and prisoner profiles via apps on their electronic devices. They can make informed decisions about leaving the area or seeking government approval to check their licensed firearm out of the public gun storage facility. Gun crime in the beyond is decreased as a result. *(See Beyond Guns, Beyond Homelessness.)*

BEYOND RELIGION/SPIRITUALITY
With Americans that grew up as students who were incentivized, rewarded, and compensated to do the right thing with an introductory right to vote...

In the beyond, "separation of church and state" remains a reality. Americans understand that separating sacred scripture from government laws allows breathing room for our founding documents so that our nation continues to evolve legally, as well as morally. Church and state are elevated by each other to a higher degree based on their commonalities. Paying taxes is likened to offering tithes. States are more proactive about encouraging citizens to believe, or even disbelieve, in order to promote national discourse about coordinating religious/spiritual outreach along with government affairs.

Americans openly practice the spiritual or religious path of their choosing as they do their culture or ethnicity. Likewise, spiritual and religious organizations highlight the efficiency and effectiveness of the government and how belief in governmental processes is akin to faith in a divine power. Just as American courts and currency state "In God We Trust," churches, temples, and mosques may state on materials promoting community resources "In the Capabilities of Positive People and Good Government We Believe."

Being incentivized and rewarded for continuously relying on a pre-ordered system of government reinforces the role divinity played in the founding of our country. Americans increasingly praise the function of an efficient and effective government that is more in tune with, and responsive to, their needs. Social ills diminish, individuals and families appreciate spiritual and religious pursuits from renewed perspectives. Exchanges between citizens and government take on more of an altruistic nature as society rewards complete spiritual and religious expression and acceptance.

Schools implement curriculums about multiple spiritual and religious practices, and encourage and incentivize students to participate in those that are most appealing to them, while having and displaying acceptance and respect for others. This future course was evident in the past with "mindfulness," yoga, and meditation being incorporated into some school systems and social settings in the early 21st century. *(See Beyond Education.)*

BEYOND REPARATIONS
With Americans that grew up as students who were incentivized, rewarded, and compensated to do the right thing with an introductory right to vote...

In the beyond, students and other Americans recognize three facts: (1) the initial idea of America, a land for all peoples, is attributed to the foresight, mental fortitude, and oppression of Europeans, the endurance of European immigrants and their immediate descendants, and this honor rests with them, who are now identified as Tru Americans; (2) the building of America and the financial rewards reaped by European descendants from harvesting its resources is attributed to the humility and resilience of Africans and their immediate descendants suffering through slave labor, the mental and spiritual fortitude and oppression of those immediate descendants without any financial gain, and the grace with which they have accepted this transgression for centuries, and this honor rests with them, who are now identified as Nu/Neo-and Indie-Americans; and (3) the initial idea of America and the building of America the nation, was done in a land where Native and other indigenous tribes and people of "color" had co-existed long before, and can be attributed to their willingness to sacrifice financial gain and ancestral ties to Earth in order that the peoples of the world could form a more perfect union, and this honor rests with them, who are now identified as Indie-Americans.

Business opportunities to sell goods and services to youth are first offered to Nu/Neo American and Indie-American business owners through the online youth marketplace/education exchange. Those descendants of slaves and indigenous tribes are offered higher compensation/wages in conjunction with additional incentives/rewards to support wealth building. In the beyond, the socioeconomic status of those communities is on par with that of their Tru-American counterparts and their descendants. In effect, an updated form of affirmative action is used to give Nu/Neo American communities the head start America owes them within the online youth market/education exchange. Tru-Americans sell most goods/services to the adult market while Nu/Neo- and Indie-Americans sell goods/services to the youth market. *(See beyond black and white, See Beyond Economics.)*

BEYOND SOCIAL SECURITY
With Americans that grew up as students who were incentivized, rewarded, and compensated to do the right thing with an introductory right to vote...

In the beyond, an online youth market/education exchange enables Americans to enter the labor force and contribute to their pension much sooner. Instead of working longer and later into life, as in the past, citizens begin earning compensation and rewards earlier in life, thus retiring earlier. Because the Social Security net has widened to take on the youth labor force, the IRS and Department of Education develop ways for younger citizens to contribute to their retirement. For example, students in daycare and pre-K earn incentives/retirement benefits for reaching developmental benchmarks such as walking or tying shoes and identifying numbers and colors. When they get older they may begin to spend their earnings and redeem rewards for their past accomplishments.

Advances in technology lead to increased job automation, decreased available jobs, and jobs that last shorter periods of time.

Americans develop more opportunities for people to contribute to their retirement fund while in school, as well as an alternative life track. The following table exemplifies how people's lives are different in the beyond regarding retirement age:

TRANSFORMATION OF TYPICAL CITIZEN LIFE TRACK	
PRESENT TRACK	**BEYOND TRACK**
(45 years of working to retirement)	(37 years of working to retirement)
Primary/Secondary Education to age 18	Primary/Secondary Education to age 16-18
College to age 22	College to age 20-22
Enter traditional workforce at age 22 for 44-45 years Work for 44-45 years until retirement 66-67 years old	Enter traditional workforce at age 20-22 **OR** enter Civic/Patriotic Duty/position at age 20-22 for 3-5 years of civil service *(rewards/compensation for positions like teacher, sanitation worker, postal worker, police officer, firefighter, etc.)*
Retirement at 66–67 years old to focus on health, family, community, education, and personal pursuits until transitioning to the Great Beyond **(TOTAL OF 45 YEARS WORKING)**	Civil Service/Patriots enter traditional workforce at ages 23-27 Work for 25 years to mid/1st retirement (optional) at age 45-52 *(based on size of retirement fund)*
	Mid/1st retirement *(optional)* at age 45-52—3 years to focus on health, family, community, education, and personal pursuits until re-entry into workforce *(incentives/rewards for Civic/Patriotic Duty positions)*
	Re-entry into workforce at age 48-55 for 12 years
	Final/2nd retirement at age 60-67 *(57 if opting out of mid/1st retirement)*—renewed focus on health, family, community, education, and personal pursuits until transitioning into the Great Beyond **(TOTAL OF 37 YEARS WORKING)**

(See Beyond Education.)

BEYOND SUBSTANCE ABUSE
With Americans that grew up as students who were incentivized, rewarded, and compensated to do the right thing with an introductory right to vote...

In the beyond, society recognizes that experimentation with substance abuse was popular among high school and college students in the past. Instead of waiting for youth to irresponsibly abuse substances on their own as youth or as adults, schools offer substance use classes. With parental and healthcare approval, students responsibly learn about, and may try, certain legal and pre-approved substances while in a safe, controlled, and structured environment with built-in rehabilitation measures. This preventive program and curriculum course is called **PRehab**, meaning to prevent rehabilitation.

Substance abuse is a thing of the past as Americans are rewarded and compensated to develop healthier habits and to avoid addictions. Based on student earnings, high-schoolers in the beyond may expect the following courses: (9th grade/PRehab 101 – sugar, caffeine, anti histamines, cough syrup, and pain relievers; 10th grade /PRehab 201 – alcohol, beer, and wine; 11th grade/PRehab 301 – marijuana, depressants, and sedatives; 12th grade/PRehab 401 – ecstasy, cocaine, and other stimulants.

Pre approval for courses depends on students meeting selection criteria in addition to paying course fees. Substance use is monitored and guided to avoid addiction and to support responsible recreational use as an adult. Students are incentivized to pass required drug screenings. Those that are ineligible to participate in high school have the option to participate later at a college or university. *(See Beyond Education.)*

BEYOND THE UNITED NATIONS
With Americans that grew up as students who were incentivized, rewarded, and compensated to do the right thing with an introductory right to vote...

In the beyond, students and other Americans recognize three important factors about the United Nations (UN): (1) the UN was founded in the United States of America; (2) the UN, headquartered in America, is an international UN-owned territory located on a piece of land carved out of New York City, wherein no federal, state, or local officer or official of the United States may enter without the consent of, and under conditions agreed to by, the UN Secretary General; and (3) the United States of America essentially is the "United Nations of America" because of the two previous factors plus the shared ideal of both entities that people of all cultures and all ethnicities from all nations around the world are welcome.

The UN implements a mission to aggressively seek a more global presence in the beyond by creating UN territories inside of each nation in the form of a large district or city. Each UN district/city requires a diverse populace with at least 100,000 residents hosted by their respective homeland nation. With the goal of bringing democracy to the whole world, citizens of the UN districts/cities are not permanent residents but temporarily reside in that UN district/city for a term of 3–5 years. During their residence, they learn a variety of mission-critical skills including, but not limited to, languages, education, business, government administration, social and economic development, and other relevant capabilities.

In addition to residing inside of their UN district/city, the temporary residents also participate in developmental exchanges outside of that UN district/city but within the country that hosts them. After their term is complete, the UN district/city temporary residents are tasked with returning to their homeland nation to implement the skills that they have learned. As residents leave their UN district/city, they make room for new temporary residents to move in and continue the mission. Over time, the populace and boundaries of each UN district/city expand within the host nation to advance democracy throughout that nation and worldwide. The UN mission is known as **VIRUS** – **V**ery **I**ntrusive **R**esolution **U**nifying **S**ociety.

BEYOND VEILED "WHITE" SUPREMACY "RACISM" & XENOPHOBIA

With Americans that grew up as students who were incentivized, rewarded, and compensated to do the right thing with an introductory right to vote...

In the beyond, students and other Americans do not hate or fear xenophobia, which includes disinformation, "white" supremacy, and the skin-color syndrome "racism." They understand xenophobia because it is contextualized through education and immigration reform. They understand that there are natural inequities and injustices in the world, from evolution through natural selection (poverty, famine, pandemics, death, etc.).

People acknowledge that fear of the unknown is what drove hate in the past when different cultures and ethnicities of the world began melting into the pot called America. Like heat, hate characteristically began to rise as those ingredients combusted. In the beyond, Americans move past xenophobia, "white" supremacy, and what had been known as "racism," but they do not do it on their own;

THEY CONTINUE TO USE A STRATEGY THAT HAD BEEN INTRODUCED BY THEIR ANCESTORS WHEN THE SKIN-COLOR SYNDROME WAS STILL BOOMING IN THE EARLY PART OF THE 21ST CENTURY...

The **B**old **E**vasive **S**trategy **T**erminating **F**anatic **R**acist **I**ncidents **E**nsuring **N**ew **D**emocracy chant was called the "BEST FRIEND" technique and simply consisted of calling "white" people "BEST FRIEND" in an attempt to de-escalate tense situations and remind "white" people that "black" and "brown" people are their partners in democracy. This innovative technique was a nod to the activism of Rev. Dr. Martin Luther King, Jr., and his nonviolent approach during our nation's turbulent civil rights' era. To counter racist attacks, "black" and "brown" people would use encounters with a "white" person as their opportunity to spread acceptance, peace, and love. Then, in the early 21st century around the 2020s, the BEST FRIEND technique was tactically executed to occasionally escape "racism" and "kill it with kindness," and people in the beyond still acknowledge the usefulness of that strategy.

Shortly after the tenure of the first elected "black" American president came to an end, strange, brutal, and unsettling phenomena began. These were not as consuming as the centuries of slavery the nation endures. Nor was it prolific as the overt lynching of "black" Americans and their "white" American sympathizers for more than half a century.

These peculiar and repetitious phenomena were allegedly benign in nature, but quickly became widespread, frustrating, and malignant. These phenomena were systemic "racism," the skin-color syndrome, including unsettling covert operations like "law" enforcement officers (typically "white) with blanket authority to perform evil hate crimes and summary executions against unarmed Americans (typically "black" and "brown"), along with "white" political representatives influencing voter intimidation/suppression and murder.

All over the country, there were countless events in which some "white" Americans were behaving in an exaggeratedly aggressive and antagonistic manner toward "black" and "brown" people. Because of the new age of social media, many of these incidents were filmed and shared around the world. Many of the assailants were actually "law" enforcement officers caught harshly questioning and attacking "black" and "brown" Americans, while conducting unnecessary traffic stops and unlawful arrests. Other incidents involved other "white" people forcefully badgering "black" and "brown" people, marginalizing them for doing their everyday tasks such as shopping, eating, or working.

Many intellectuals at the time had chalked up these rapidly reoccurring routines to "'white' backlash," an animosity on the part of some "white" Americans, who were angered by the electing of an openly "black" person as our president. The intellectuals were not wrong, but they did not have the entire story. These ominous and repetitive occurrences had also begun to happen at a time when a highly secretive and sinister organization coded Q-Anon and devoted to disinformation, including "white" supremacy, conspiracy theories, and violent "racism," was gaining mass popularity online among xenophobes. Even a former U.S. president and supporter of Q-Anon succeeded at spreading the "huge" lie about winning an election that he lost. The coordinators behind this menacing movement were unknown for a time but, eventually their identities were uncovered, and their diabolical motives revealed.

Although shocked and awed, Americans were not surprised to learn that the Q-Anon coordinators were using the name of their xenophobic, conspiracy-theory–driven organization as a coded call-to-action for people afflicted with the skin color syndrome, "racism." The name Q-Anon itself had a three-layered meaning only known to its members.

The first layer of the Q-Anon code meant "Cue [Q] to anonymously [Anon] express your 'racism.'" Because using racial slurs was an obvious signal that someone was "racist," Q-Anon coordinated A\WAY online to anonymously express, manifest, and spread hate throughout America.

The second layer of the code was a sub-acronym that was kept in secret by its members to avoid the perspective that Q-Anon was an overtly racist organization. As a call to violently attack "black" and "brown" people, **Q-Anon** stood for "**Q**uestion **A**ll 'Niggers' **O**ppressively **N**ow." This coded call was only directed to "white," male "law" enforcement officials to legally stop "black" and "brown" people and harass them in A\WAY to make them feel less than human in their own country.

The third layer spoke to the motives behind Q-Anon, which was to provide A\WAY for women who were also afflicted with "racism," the skin-color syndrome. The Q-Anon women were responsible for employing other coded techniques such as KAREN, which had two alternate meanings: (a) "Keep Attacking Real Everyday 'Niggers'" and (b) "Keep Attacking Real Exemplary 'Niggers.'" So, whether it was a "black" or "brown" person deemed of average standing or stellar accomplishment, they were criminalized through malicious verbal, mental, and emotional assaults that sometimes became malevolent physical attacks.

Once the naked truth about Q-Anon was exposed, "black" and "brown" Americans, and their allies, responded with an acronym like Q-Anon and KAREN—"BEST FRIEND"—as one of their peaceful strategies to combat the pervasive and xenophobic onslaught, eerily reminiscent to the Ku Klux Klan. That link is blatantly obvious by the very lettering: [K]**Q-A**non; [K]AREN (a); [K]AREN (b) = KKK.

After several years, the Q-Anon movement had begun to dissolve. Despite best efforts, the skin-color syndrome could not be eliminated. A then-future U.S. senator from Great Britain, realizing that hate could not be erased from every human heart, but that democracy would not be denied, made another arrangement, and by 2026, America's 250th anniversary, "Brexit II" and "Brexit III" were well underway.

The term "Brexit" was coined during a past political/economic conflict on the continent of Europe. Previously, the European countries unified monetarily and were using one single currency, the Euro. After several years, one country, Great Britain, wanted to back out of the agreement. That country's eventual departure and the preceding events are historically called "Brexit," the British exit.

Later, the future senator and their spouse, both members of the British Royal family, involved in a skin-color-syndrome marriage scandal, exited Great Britain, "Brexit II," and gave up their royal duties, moving their growing family to the United States of America. By 2026, the senator, now cofirmed at this point, advocates for "Brexit III," groundbreaking immigration reform resulting in two major pieces of legislation and manifesting in two new international migratory patterns: the **SHIFT** Act; and the "Reverse-Immigration" bill.

The SHIFT (**S**ome **H**ead **I**nto **F**rench **T**erritory) was a new migratory pattern resulting from Americans being incentivized, rewarded, and compensated to seek out new economic opportunities in Canada. NAFTA (the North American Free Trade Agreement) is amended and becomes **NAFTTA**, the **N**orth **A**merican **F**ree **T**rade and **T**ravel **A**greement. This change allows an increased number of citizens in North America and the Caribbean to travel with increased freedom between any two North American countries. Many "black" and "brown" Central and Caribbean American citizens find jobs in the U.S., prompting the "shift" of "white" Americans up into neighboring Canada.

The Reverse-Immigration bill also legally arranges for people unsettled by the natural influx of "black/brown" people into the United States as a result of SHIFT to be incentivized, rewarded, and compensated to immigrate to Great Britain, the other nation representing said senator's dual citizenship. A symbiotic economic relationship is established as "white" Americans that migrate rent out their U.S. properties to "black" and "brown" Central/Caribbean (Immi-American) citizens that also migrate during the year.

THESE NEW MIGRATORY PATTERNS LEAD TO THE ESTABLISHMENT OF THE WORLD'S FIRST MAJOR TRANSIT ROUTES AS PEOPLE BEGIN TO FREQUENTLY TRAVEL THE GLOBE USING INTERNATIONAL SPACE TRANSIT, IN THE BEYOND.

(See Beyond Immigration.)

It is a reverse form of immigration that, perhaps, the founders of our democracy had envisioned...

CHAPTER

CONCLUSION (THE UNKOWN)

...from the inception of our great nation when the entire world was plunged into the unknown. How could our founders have known exactly what the future would hold with a land open to every ethnicity, every culture and peoples from around the globe. For nearly the past 250 years American citizens have been exploring this unknown ideal, this concept of racial, ethnic, and religious harmony. And while there have been successes along the way, things are once again at a boiling point.

No doubt, the centuries of strife in America are due to the duality of human emotion. At once we are beings filled with the propensity to love and simultaneously consumed by hate. The hate is what leads us back to strife, conflict, and tension. The love is what fuels us to success, victory, and triumph. All other nations are waiting for America to figure out how to lessen the hate within our own borders so that our beacon of true democracy may shine to the entire world and we can all love one another.

But how DO we lessen the hate? How DO we encourage one another to diminish the racist, bigoted, and prejudiced views we may hold for people different from ourselves? This may seem particularly difficult when we instinctively learn these behaviors from our elders. But the solution lies in our past, in actions we have already been doing. We DO it by training and rewarding ourselves, our youth, and each other to do the right thing. It will become clearer when we think about the following unknowns:

Where would we be...

If children never got ice cream, candy, and allowances to do their chores?

Where would we be...

If employees never got paid to show up to work?

Where would we be...

If corporations never got tax breaks to create more jobs?

Where would we be...

If dogs never got treats to sit and roll over?

Where would we be...?

We would be stuck. We would be stuck in a world without progress. But fortunately, we don't live in that world. We live in America where progress is the norm. We do reward children for chores and they learn to clean up. We do pay employees and they show up to get the job done. We do offer corporations incentives to create more jobs and it leads to stronger, more prosperous communities. And we do give dogs treats when they sit and roll over and they are our best friends.

So, the same can be said for curbing ethnic and cultural hatred and accomplishing the near impossible task of creating a diverse society free of injustice and inequity. We must train and reward people, especially in their youth, to do the right thing. More specifically, to do what the framers of the Constitution envisioned. And we must train and reward them with incentives for proper behavior just like we've been doing with children and chores, employees at work, and dogs and tricks.

T.H.E. A.N.S.W.E.R. has been in our past, at our feet all along. Just like the famed novel *The Wonderful Wizard of Oz* and its' main character, Dorothy, lost in a land called OZ, it's time for America to simply click her heels three times and go home to her destiny.

Let's go home everyone, at the count of three...
1. Pay
2. The
3. Kids

Again...
1 Let
2. Students
3. Vote

One more time...
1. Incentivize
2. Good
3. Behavior

... And when we get there, to the great beyond, to a new world where social injustice and inequity have been greatly diminished, the biggest unknown we may face could be learning how to live without them.

APPENDIX

POTENTIAL
HEADLINES FROM
THE
TEEN NEW DEAL

POTENTIAL HEADLINES FROM THE TEEN NEW DEAL

JANUARY
- "Student Lives Matter Now Trending"
- "U.S. High School & Middle School Students Stage Virtual Protests Interrupting Online Learning – Demand Teen New Deal, Education Labor, & Nationwide Student Governments"

FEBRUARY
- "Foreign Youth Activists Pledge Support For American Youth Protests & Teen New Deal"
- "Crown Prince Of Saudi Arabia Reiterates Silicon Valley Speech of 2020, Youth of His Country Ready to Work"

MARCH
- "Major U.S. Cities Announce Plan to Follow DC's Lead, Will Extend Summer Youth Employment Programs Into Fall"

APRIL
- "DC Mayor Stays One Step Ahead of the Pack, Announces Decision to Extend Summer Youth Employment Program Thru Winter With Limited Number Of Youth Participants"

MAY
- "Youth Protest For Teen New Deal Go Offline & Into Streets, Parents Join in Saying Families Could Benefit"

JUNE
- "U.S. Conference of Mayors (USCM) Pens Letter To U.S. Dept. Of Ed Requesting Student Government Be Mandated in All Public Schools"

JULY
- "National Student Council (NATSTUCO) Weighs In on Student Government Debate, Says They Have Capacity to Help Set Up Nationwide SGAs"

AUGUST
- "U.S. Secretary Of Education Announces Plan To Mandate Nationwide Student Governments For High School & Middle School By Fall '22 – Will Begin With Write-In Campaigns & Selection Committees In Spring '22"

SEPTEMBER
- "U.S. Congress Forms Exploratory Commission On Youth Pay & Digital Currency, Will Reveal Findings In 6 Months"
- "U.S. Youth Protests For Teen New Deal Resume Online Disrupting Virtual Classrooms"

OCTOBER
- "U.S. Secretary of Education Makes Another Bold Move, Mandates Student Government for Elementary Schools by Fall '23— Write-In Campaigns to Begin Early '23"

NOVEMBER
- "U.S. College Athletes Support Youth Protests Online, Say That Education Labor Will Lead To College Athletes Being Paid"

DECEMBER
- "Youth Activism At All Time High Around The World. Kids Say All They Want For Christmas Is A Teen New Deal!"

POTENTIAL HEADLINES FROM THE TEEN NEW DEAL

JANUARY
- "Major Hedge Fund Founder Announces Plan to Finance Student Government for DC High Schools Beginning Fall '22, Will Pay Youth Stipends With Digital Currency"

FEBRUARY
- "Coalition Of U.S. Media Corporations Announce Plan to Adopt Select U.S. School Districts to Model 'Teen New Deal', Will Seek To Develop Closed Circuit TV Networks For High Schools"
- "Write-In Campaigns For Student Government Positions Begin For High School & Middle School"

MARCH
- "U.S. President Announces Findings of Congressional Committee on Youth Pay & Digital Currency, Says A Teen New Deal Could Be Signed Into Law By Summer 2024"

APRIL
- "DC Mayor Says Summer Youth Employment Program in Nation's Capital Will Be First to Go Year-Round In 2023 With Limited Youth Participation"

MAY
- "Stock Market Gains Attributed To Media Stocks & Financial Backing of Student Governments With Cryptocurrency"
- "Investment In Digital Currency Through The Roof"

JUNE
- "Major U.S. Cities Try to Keep Pace With DC, Will Extend Summer Youth Employment Programs Into Winter '23"

JULY
- "U.S. Treasury Secretary & Banking Chief Partner With Secretary of Ed to Pay New Teachers With Digital Currency Starting Fall '23, Will Use Distributed Ledger Software Known as Blockchain"

- "U.S. President Reveals Plan for Teen New Deal, Says Should Be Signed by Spring '23 in 3-Phase Rollout"
- "U.S. Social Security Admin, IRS, & Dept Of Ed In Talks to Set Student Wage Structure, Parent & Corporate Incentives"

AUGUST
- "U.S. Congress Set to Revise Fair Labor Standards Act to Include Child Labor Under Age 16"
- "U.S. Congress to Renew National Youth Administration as Independent Funding Arm of Dept of Ed, Will Seek Corporate Pledges & Contributions of at Least $100 Billion"

SEPTEMBER
- "U.S. President to Address United Nations About the Benefits of the Teen New Deal"
- "U. S. Youth Protests For Teen New Deal Resume Online Disrupting Virtual Classrooms"

OCTOBER
- "Opposition To Teen New Deal By Religious & Parent Advocacy Groups, Say Children Will Be Exploited"
- "U.s. Civil Rights Organizations Say Teen New Deal Could Be Alternate Route to Reparations for Black & Native American Communities"

NOVEMBER
- "U.S. & Foreign Corporations Lining Up to Pledge to National Youth Administration Fund, Pledges Nearing $100 Billion Goal"

DECEMBER
- "French President Reveals Design of New Sculptural Gift to United States In Recognition of Teen New Deal & Youth Liberation, Statue of Destiny Could Be Complete In 2 Years"

POTENTIAL HEADLINES FROM THE TEEN NEW DEAL

JANUARY
- "D.C. & Several Major U.S. Cities Kickoff First Year Of Year-Round Youth Employment Programs, With Limited Youth Participation"
- "Senate & House debate TEEN NEW DEAL Components & Legislation"

FEBRUARY
- "Plans for TEEN NEW DEAL Appear Filibuster-Proof in U.S. Congress"
- "Student Write-in Campaigns for Elementary Student Governments to Begin in U.S."

MARCH
- "U.S. Cryptocurrency Investment Continues to Rise"
- "Dozens of Major U.S. Retailers Now Accepting Digital Currency"

APRIL
- "TEEN NEW DEAL Approved by U.S. Congress, Signed Into Law as Education Labor Act!"
- "U.S. Federal Government Contracts With Private Tech Firm to Build/ Maintain Online Youth Markets aka Education Exchanges; Feds Will Provide Oversight"

MAY
- "Corporate Contributions to U.S. National Youth Administration Fund Top $100 Billion"
- "U.S. Education Labor Act Mandates Digital Divide Between Adult & Youth Content; Users Must Access Internet With National ID"
- "U.S. Dept of Ed & Corporations Finalize Incentive/Rewards-Based Curriculums"

JUNE
- "U.S. Congress Passes Affirmative Wages Act; Black & Native American Students Will Earn Higher Wage For 25 Years"

- "Online Youth Market Training Begins in U.S.; Principals, Teachers, & Student Government Members Learn How to Distribute Earnings/ Incentives to Students"

JULY
- "Students Throughout U.S. Receiving National ID Cards Tied to Social Security"
- "Students & Parents in U.S. to Begin Pre-Registration on Online Youth Markets, Students Will Start Earning in October"

AUGUST
- "U.S. Federal Government Begins Installation Of Closed-Circuit TV Equipment Inside Schools, Y.E.T.– *Youth Education TV*—To Begin Broadcasting Fall '24"

SEPTEMBER
- "U.S. Student Governments in Effect Nationwide, SGA Members Taking Part in Educating Students About Details of Online Youth Markets"

OCTOBER
- "U.S. Students Now Earning Pre-Credit For Online Youth Market; Can't Spend Earnings Until Summer '24"
- "U.S. Affirmative Wages Act Mandates Black & Native American Students Earn Higher Wage for 25 Years"

NOVEMBER
- "Foreign Investment in Digital Currency Soars In International Markets"

DECEMBER
- "D.C. & Several Major U.S. Cities Celebrate Full Year of Year-Round Employment For Teens"
- "U.S. Youth Employment Programs Will Be Re-Evaluated In Light of Education Labor Act"

POTENTIAL HEADLINES FROM THE TEEN NEW DEAL

JANUARY
- "French President Says Construction of Statue of Destiny on schedule For Xmas '24"

FEBRUARY
- "Media Conglomerates Offer Feds Big Bucks For Broadcasting Rights On Y.E.T. (Youth Education Television), The U.S. Closed Circuit TV Network"

MARCH
- "U.S. Department of Health & Human Services Attributes Last Quarter '23 Dip in Nationwide Teen Pregnancy to Teen New Deal Incentives"

APRIL
- "U.S. Student Government Associations Gear Up for Annual Elections; School Security at Top of Most Student Voter Lists"

MAY
- "U.S. Online Youth Market Launches Full Steam Ahead!"
- "U.S. Students & Parents Ready To Spend Previous School Year Earnings On Everything From Books & Uniform Fashions to Utilities & Investments"
- "Corporations With Biggest Pledges to U.S. National Youth Admin Fund Are Top Retailers in Online Youth Market"

JUNE
- "Annual G-7 Summit Meets in Italy; Member Leaders to Discuss How to Bring Education Labor to World Markets"
- "Online Youth Market Training Begins in U.S.; Principals, Teachers, & Student Government Members Learn How to Distribute Earnings/ Incentives to Students"

JULY
- "U.S. Parent Advocacy Groups Objecting to Content Being Produced For YET, Say Too Mature For Students"

AUGUST
- "U.S. Teachers Say Behavior Management Much More Effective Due to Education Labor Act; Teachers Can Finally Teach Instead of Babysit"
- "U.S. Students Ready to Get Back to School & Earn"

SEPTEMBER
- "United Nations Security Council Says Worldwide TEEN NEW DEALS & Organized Education Labor Crucial To World Peace & Economic Stability"
- "U.S. Youth Education TV (Y.E.T.) Begins Broadcasting In U.s. Schools, Corporations With Largest Pledges To NYA Fund Are Top Advertisers"

OCTOBER
- "Teen pregnancy in U.S. Continues to Decline for 4th Straight Quarter"
- "U.S. Department of Education Releases First Report on Student Earnings, Female Students Are Highest Earners!"

NOVEMBER
- "G-7 Invites Russia & China to Sign, Will Soon Become A Gang Of Nine"
- "U.S. Adoption Rates Increase Dramatically, Foster Homes/ Orphanages Empty Out as Parents Try to Take Advantage of Education Labor Act Benefits"

DECEMBER
- "Statue of Destiny Arrives in San Francisco Bay"

ABOUT THE AUTHOR

Sidney Nordé is an educator, author, and theoretician. He is a co-founder of the Do The Write Thing Foundation of DC, a youth-based non-profit focused on media literacy. His other work includes research and publication of an independent discovery, **TIE** – Theory of Interplanetary Evolution – an expansion of Charles Darwin's work on evolution, combined with data from NASA.

His newest project, *A Manifesto for Americans – THE ANSWER*, suggests how the United States can prepare for the instability of future pandemics and begin to move past long-standing racial conflict by building an alternative economy for teenagers using an Online Youth Marketplace. He believes that if students are paid with a digital currency and rewarded to make better decisions, young people can be incentivized into becoming champions of justice and true American democracy.